LAW OFFICES OF
MICHAEL J. GOPIN, PLLC.

PERSONAL INJURY CASES IN TEXAS

Everything You Need To Know
Before And After Filing Your Claim

MICHAEL J. GOPIN, ESQ.
LEE R. MONTION, ESQ.

Jacobs & Whitehall
73-03 Bell Blvd, #10
Oakland Gardens, NY 11364
www.jacobsandwhitehall.com
Ordering Information:

Quantity sales. Special discounts are available on quantity purchases by corporations, associations, and others. For details, contact the publisher at the address above.

Orders by U.S. trade bookstores and wholesalers. Please contact Jacobs & Whitehall: Tel: (888) 991-2766 or visit www.jacobsandwhitehall.com.

Printed in the United States of America

Published in 2020

ISBN: 978-1-951149-32-1

PREFACE

The Law Offices of MJG, PLLC is focused on taking care of our community and offering our assistance whenever necessary. With 30+ years of experience in the area of personal injury, our goal for this book is to inform and educate the public on all areas of personal injury.

DEDICATION

To our wives Dawn and Jessica. Behind every successful man is a woman who makes it all happen.

We would also like to dedicate this book to the first responders, victims and their families of the tragic Walmart shootings that took place in El Paso, Texas. #elpasostrong

DISCLAIMER

This publication is intended to be used for educational purposes only. No legal advice is being given, and no attorney-client relationship is intended to be created by reading this material. The author assumes no liability for any errors or omissions or for how this book or its contents are used or interpreted, or for any consequences resulting directly or indirectly from the use of this book. For legal or any other advice, please consult an experienced attorney or the appropriate expert, who is aware of the specific facts of your case and is knowledgeable in the law in your jurisdiction.

Law Offices of
Michael J. Gopin, PLLC.
1300 El Paso St
El Paso, Texas 79902
(915) 233-1747
www.michaelgopin.com

TESTIMONIALS

"I was badly injured in an accident and the insurance was refusing to pay. Michael Gopin settled my case and got my car fixed, medical bills paid and I got a great settlement too. The staff was caring and attentive to me. I couldn't be happier. Go see Michael Gopin."

– Alfredo

****

"I was in bad shape when I hired Michael Gopin. He and his staff quickly took care of my issues and settled my case. I am beyond happy with their services."

– Pam

****

"Wonderful staff and attorney. Michael Gopin took the time to explain all the facts and details regarding my case. My case was settled quickly for a great amount. All my bills were paid."

– Mary

****

"The staff and Michael Gopin were totally professional and caring. My case settled and I received an excellent settlement. This office cared about me. Thanks, Michael Gopin. I highly recommend."

– Jorge

****

"Awesome settlement. Everything smooth and easy. They fought hard for me and negotiated large discounts on my medical bills."

– Frank

****

TABLE OF CONTENTS

8

9

ABOUT THE AUTHORS

Michael J. Gopin

Michael J. Gopin is the name behind the firm and the author of this book. Michael graduated from the University of Texas at Austin, attended law school at St. Mary's University in San Antonio, Texas, and became licensed to practice in the state of Texas in 1987.

Michael has practiced law in El Paso since 1987. Even after more than 30 years, he still remembers his first jury case. Two weeks after receiving his license, he represented a person whose life had been forever changed after being blinded in a work-related incident. "We convinced the jury to agree with us and received a favorable verdict," he remembers.

This victory has stuck with him as justice was served. He is proud that he continues to build a long list of satisfied clients. Michael has successfully handled countless cases of medical malpractice, product liability, personal injury, and nursing home negligence. He enjoys helping people "get their lives back in order" by providing high-quality legal representation and compassionate customer service.

Michael especially likes leveling the playing field for individuals who find themselves in disputes against huge insurance companies. His law firm has earned a reputation for having the experience and the resources to go to fight large insurers that try to delay, deny, or devalue legitimate claims.

In his spare time, Michael is a devoted family man, plays competitive table tennis and travels the world. He has been to all continents in the world except Antartica. Michael and his wife Dawn have several children and he he hopes one or more may study law.

Lee R. Montion

Lee R. Montion, the co-author of this book and partner at the Law Offices of Michael Gopin, PLLC. is an El Paso native. Lee Montion didn't start his career in the field of personal injury law. In fact, his compassion for individuals and families struggling to cope with tragedy began when he worked as a funeral director earlier in his career. He saw families trying to pick up the pieces and make important decisions after tragic, life-altering events. This is why he knows how crucial it is to have a steady, guiding hand during difficult times.

Like many people, Lee's first experience with the law was through television. He watched the TV series L.A. Law of the late 1980s and early 1990s with his mom. He graduated from the University of Texas at El Paso in 2000 with a bachelor's degree in marketing before working in the funeral business for six years. Eventually, he decided to follow his calling and earned his Juris Doctorate from Texas A&M School of Law in 2009.

There are many aspects of Lee's job that he enjoys. But mostly, he loves helping people. "When people are hurt and they can't work and don't know how they're going to pay their bills, they're in a pretty stressful time of need," he says. Lee knows what a difference he can make in these people's lives. He and the legal team at the Law Offices of Michael J. Gopin, PLLC, work hard to take the pressure off clients, answer their questions, and give them confidence that their case is in good hands.

In his leisure time, Lee plays golf. He is happily married to Jessica with two kids, a boy and a girl, and another boy on the way.

Why Are You Writing This Book? What Do You Want Readers To Gain From This?

In writing this book, our goal is to help the public better understand the legal process of personal injury cases and how to protect themselves from the many traps set by insurance companies. Contrary to what some people believe, attempting to handle a personal injury claim without the help of an experienced personal injury lawyer can prevent a person from obtaining the compensation they need and deserve. Our hope is that this book shows the many ways in which a personal injury lawyer can benefit those who are pursuing a personal injury claim.

CHAPTER 1

TYPES OF PERSONAL INJURY CASES WE HANDLE

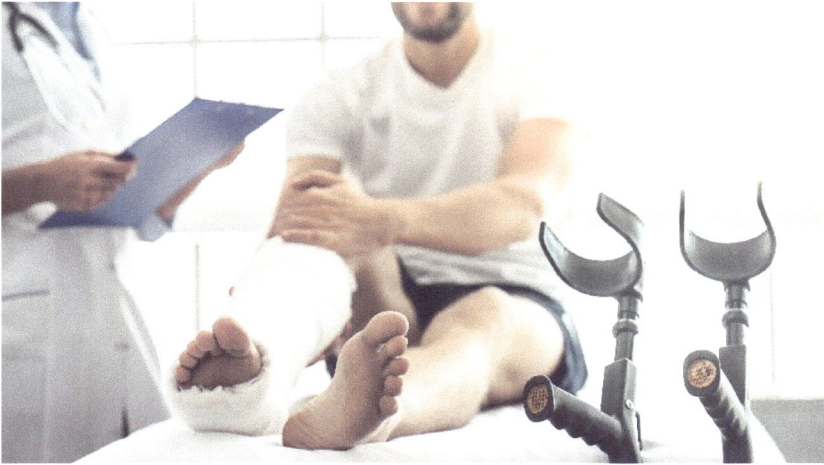

We most commonly handle personal injury cases involving automobile accidents, trucking accidents, and slip-and-fall accidents. However, we also handle mass tort cases (e.g. 3M earplug, hernia mesh, Roundup, and e-cigarette types of cases).

When Does A Personal Injury Claim Arise In Texas?

A personal injury lawsuit arises when a person sustains an injury due to the negligence of another person.

These injuries can be physical, emotional, and financial in nature, and often result in physical impairment, pain and suffering, significant medical bills, and lost wages.

Critical First Steps After An Accident Or Injury

If you have been injured in an accident, the first thing you should do is seek medical attention; any delay in doing so could potentially harm your case. There are a few critical steps you should take in order to ensure that you wind up with the strongest possible case, the first of which is to gather key information at the scene of the accident (e.g. the name and phone number of the persons who caused the accident and any witnesses, insurance policy information, and photos of the vehicles involved in the accident).

You should abstain from giving a statement to the insurance company and instead make sure that you have legal representation who can take care of that on your behalf. You should not accept blame for the accident or tell anyone that you are not injured. Oftentimes, a person will not notice an injury or pain until a day or two after an accident, so making a premature statement about whether or not you've been hurt could end up hurting your case. It is important to avoid posting on social media, as doing so could invalidate your personal injury claim. It is best to keep everything private; the insurance company will investigate you through all possible channels and use anything they can against you.

CHAPTER 2

PASSENGER VEHICLE ACCIDENTS VERSUS TRUCKING ACCIDENTS

Trucking accidents are much more complex than car accidents, in part because the transportation industry is regulated at the state and federal level. There are several potential causes of trucking accidents, including poor vehicle maintenance, unqualified drivers, and vehicle defects. It's important to hire an attorney who is experienced in these matters and knows how to obtain the strongest evidence in support of your claim.

Potentially Liable Parties In A Large Semi-Truck Or Other Commercial Vehicle Accident

Among the many possible defendants in a trucking accident case, there is the driver of the truck, the trucking company, the maintenance company, the manufacturer of the vehicle, and the party responsible for loading the cargo on the truck. Trucking accident cases are complicated and require the expertise of a lawyer who has handled hundreds of them before.

Type Of Evidence Most Helpful In Trucking Accident Cases

The type of evidence that is most helpful in a trucking accident case will depend on the facts unique to the particular case at hand. Accident reconstruction experts, medical experts, witnesses, economists, and life planners might be required or beneficial depending on the nature of a case.

Why Do I Need An Attorney Who Has Dealt Specifically With Trucking Accident Cases?

Trucking accident cases involve various complex issues and considerations, such as whether or not the trucking company hired an unqualified driver or allowed a driver to become overworked or fatigued, whether or not the truck had undergone the required maintenance checks, and whether or not the truck was loaded properly. If it can be demonstrated that the trucking company violated a state or federal regulation, then a case could become tremendously valuable. For this reason, it's important to hire an experienced trucking accident lawyer who is well-versed in these issues.

CHAPTER 3

TYPES OF INJURIES MOTORCYCLE RIDERS SUSTAIN

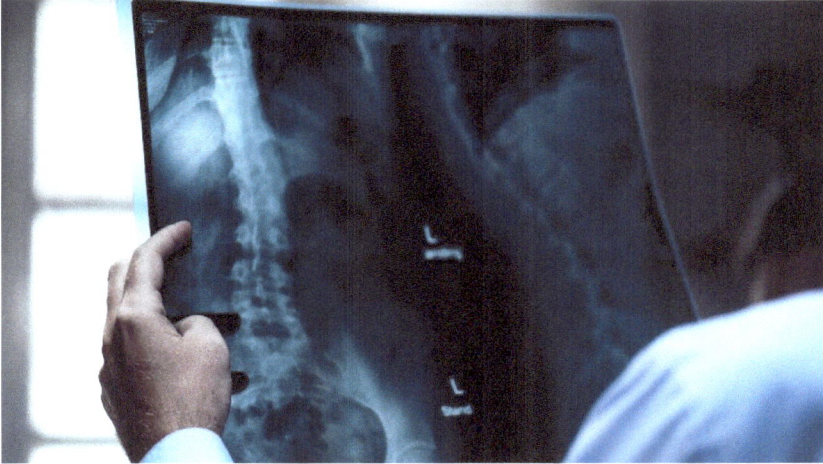

Common types of injuries suffered in motorcycle accidents include road rash, facial fractures and disfigurement, broken bones, and burns. Injuries can range from minor to catastrophic, including traumatic brain injuries, amputation, spinal cord injuries, and paralysis.

Challenges In Motorcycle Accident-Related Personal Injury Claims

Unfortunately, there is a bias against motorcycle riders; if you've been injured while riding a motorcycle, it's important that your lawyer is aware of this bias, and does everything they can to mitigate it by putting you in the best possible light. It's also important to eliminate jurors who may be particularly biased against motorcycle riders, which is why the questioning process for a jury is critical, and ensuring that there is a fair and equitable jury is essential. Another challenge is that the damages suffered by motorcycle riders usually far exceed the available minimal policy limits in Texas, and to worsen matters, many motorcycle riders don't carry underinsured motorist coverage.

How Will Having Worn (Or Not Worn) Safety Gear Affect My Motorcycle Accident Claim?

In Texas, anyone who is under the age of 21 is required to wear a helmet while riding a motorcycle, but anyone who is over the age of 21 is not required to wear a helmet after they have completed a motorcycle operating training course or can provide at least $10,000 in medical insurance coverage. However, failure to use a helmet can have a negative impact on your case, because the insurance company can blame you for not mitigating your injuries by protecting yourself with the use of a helmet.

Benefits Of Hiring An Attorney Experienced In Handling Motorcycle Accident Cases

A well-trained and experienced attorney in motorcycle-related personal injury cases can make a huge difference, as the type of injuries sustained and the ability to understand how a motorcycle accident occurs is essential. Understanding the unique perspectives of a motorcyclist is also important.

CHAPTER 4

PREMISES LIABILITY LAWS AND SLIP-AND-FALL CASES

The legal standard for slip-and-fall cases in Texas is that the property or store owner must have had actual or constructive notice of the dangerous condition, meaning that they should have known about the dangerous condition before the accident happened.

How To Determine That A Property Owner Should Have Known Of A Dangerous Condition?

Proving that a store or property owner should have known about a dangerous condition is a difficult task that depends heavily upon circumstantial evidence. For example, if there was an object or a spill in the middle of a grocery store aisle, it would be important to determine how long it had been there before the slip-and-fall occurred, and how often the store owner checked the aisles for safety hazards. If there was evidence of shoeprints near a spill, then that would indicate that another person had already walked through the spill. If a piece of fruit caused a slip-and-fall, examining the piece of fruit itself could indicate roughly how long it had been there.

If it can be shown to a jury that a safety hazard was present for a long period of time, then it will be easier to argue that the store or property owner should have known about it. Many stores will have video footage, which could either help or hurt your case. For example, if the video footage shows that a spill remained on the floor for several hours before the slip-and-fall incident, then that would work in your favor; if the video footage shows that the spill occurred just minutes prior to the slip-and-fall incident, then that would help the store owner by showing that they couldn't have reasonably been aware of the dangerous condition.

Impact Of Comparative Negligence In Slip-And-Fall Cases

Comparative negligence has a major impact on slip-and-fall personal injury cases in Texas. Oftentimes, a store or property owner will argue that you were negligent by not watching where you were going, and that you should have seen and avoided the safety hazard. Another tactic used by store or property owners is to claim that the slip-and-fall incident occurred only because the type of shoe you were wearing (e.g. high heels as opposed to boots).

If it can be shown that you were more than 50 percent at fault for your injury, then the claim will be barred. Store or property owners will try to place as much blame on you as possible in order to pay less in damages.

Steps To Consider In Making A Slip-And-Fall Personal Injury Claim

If you've been involved in a slip-and-fall accident, one of the first things you should do is take photos of the dangerous condition which caused you to fall. Next, you should report the injury to the store manager, as well as collect useful information such as the names and phone numbers of any witnesses and the store employees. After that, you should immediately seek medical attention. Do not provide a statement of the event to the insurance company; instead, call our office any time of the day or night and we will advise you on how to proceed.

CHAPTER 5

IMPORTANT PHASES OF A PERSONAL INJURY CLAIM

In Texas, a personal injury claim is divided into several phases. After the injury, you should contact an attorney and tell them about the incident, and the attorney should then notify the insurance company of the incident. The insurance company will send out preliminary letters and begin processing the claim. At this point, property damage claims will be presented to the company. Oftentimes, the insurance company requests to inspect the vehicle and make a statement of our version of the facts.

In the meantime, you will consult the healthcare provider of your choice. The length of treatment will depend on the severity of the injury. Once you have concluded treatment, all of the medical records and bills will be gathered and reviewed by the attorney's office. At this point, the case will be ready for negotiations and you will meet with your attorney to discuss the value and merits of the case. Once you reach an agreement, your attorney will try to successfully negotiate a settlement on your behalf. If the negotiations are not settled at that point, then the alternative would be to file a lawsuit in court and litigate the case to a conclusion.

Statute Of Limitations

The statute of limitations for a personal injury claim in Texas is two years from the date of the accident. There are several exceptions, including federal tort claims and cases involving minors. In addition, there are notice requirements that need to be followed for cases involving state and city entities.

Significance Of Evidence And Witnesses

Preservation of evidence from the scene of an auto or slip-and-fall accident is crucial to a personal injury case, which is why it's a good idea to take pictures of the vehicles involved in an accident or the dangerous condition which led to a slip-and-fall accident. In the event of an auto accident, pictures of the other driver, their insurance card, and their driver's license should also be taken, and a report should be filed with the police department. In any type of personal injury case, keeping detailed witness information is extremely important for a valid and strong claim.

How Does Comparative Fault Impact A Personal Injury Case?

Comparative fault or negligence will definitely affect your recovery. If you are deemed to be more than 50 percent at fault for an accident, recovery will be barred. If you are deemed 50 percent or less at fault, then you will receive a percentage of damages inversely proportional to the percentage of fault. For example, if an accident was 30 percent your fault and the jury awarded $10,000, then the claim would be reduced by 30 percent of the total, to $7,000.

CHAPTER 6

SHOULD I GO FOR A SETTLEMENT OR A CASE TRIAL?

There are many important factors that an attorney will look at when determining whether or not a case should be settled, including all pros and cons, the length of time it will take to get to trial, the cost of trial, risk versus reward, and how you are likely to be perceived by a jury.

How Time-Consuming And Costly Are Trials In Personal Injury Cases?

If a case goes to trial, it will add several years to the timeline and substantially increase costs. The cost will depend upon the complexity of the case, depositions, expert witnesses needed to properly litigate the case, and the amount of paperwork involved. Generally, the higher the potential judgment, the greater the cost of litigation.

Hiring An Attorney Versus Going It Alone

Hiring an experienced personal injury attorney will dramatically increase the likelihood of getting a better settlement, and we strongly advise against handling a case alone. There are so many pitfalls along the way that clients don't even know to look out for, and always remember that the insurance companies are not your friend or on your side.

CHAPTER 7

HOW ARE SETTLEMENT AMOUNTS CALCULATED IN TEXAS?

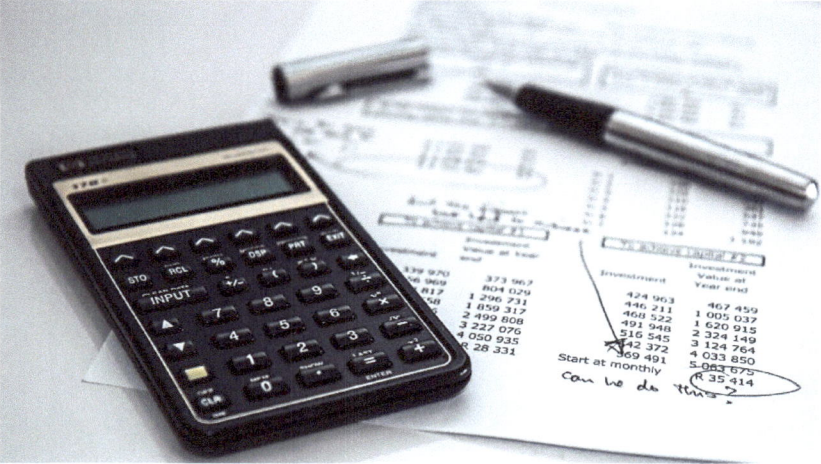

There is no set method for calculating settlement amounts; such determinations are made on a case-by-case basis and depend on a number of factors, such as the amount of medical bills, the severity of the injuries, and lost wages. The future impact of the injury also plays an important role in cases involving severe injuries. Oftentimes, an expert witness will be needed in order to determine future medical bills and future economic impact in cases of serious injury. For instance, if you were not able to work for an extended period of time past the trial date, then you should receive substantial economic damages in the future. There are also general damages for pain and suffering and lost wages, but you and your attorney hold the burden of proof for these damages. For example, in order to obtain a certain amount of compensation for lost wages, we will have to provide proof of lost wages and other information from your employer, including past tax returns.

How Is The Amount Of Monetary Recovery Determined?

Monetary recovery is determined by many different factors in a personal injury case, such as the liability issue of the defendant, the severity of the injury, and the limits of the insurance policy.

How Will I Pay For Ongoing Medical Expenses?

Ongoing medical expenses can be paid using several different sources. Using health insurance is always a good option for paying medical bills. In many cases, doctors and other healthcare professionals will work on a letter of protection or lien in the case, which will prevent you from having to pay for medical services until the case has been resolved. An experienced personal injury lawyer will know which doctors will accept letters of protection and will be able to direct you to the appropriate medical care facility.

Who Recoups Funds After The Settlement?

Upon settlement of a case, the insurance company will send a check and a release to your attorney. After that, the funds will be deposited into a trust account. The attorney will draft a disbursement agreement which outlines the manner in which the funds are to be divided. The medical bills and the amount that you will recover will be paid from the trust account, and all of this information will be documented in the disbursement agreement.

Does A More Severe Injury Increase The Chances Of A Larger Settlement?

While it's not the only factor, having sustained a severe injury can lead to a larger settlement. The liability of the defendant is an equally important issue, because questionable liability can substantially reduce the value of a possible settlement.

How Will A Traffic Ticket Impact My Case?

Receiving a ticket due to an auto accident may not be a big problem. The responders did not witness the accident and will therefore only be going by their assessment at the time of the trial. Many times, a ticket will be dismissed and will not directly affect a case. However, if you were ticketed for a safety issue, such as failure to use a seatbelt, then the defendant could use that fact to argue that you wouldn't have sustained an injury had you been wearing a seatbelt. The same argument would be used if a motorcyclist sustained a head injury while not wearing a helmet.

CHAPTER 8

TACTICS INSURANCE COMPANIES USE TO AVOID PAYING OUT ON CLAIMS

There are many different defenses an insurance company can use to avoid paying claims. One of the most common defenses is to blame you, the injured party, by arguing that you were at fault for the accident. Another tactic used by insurance companies is to claim that their insured is not cooperating with the investigation. In certain situations, they might claim that the person who was driving was not covered under the policy or there was a lapse in coverage due to non-payment of the insurance premium.

Should I Notify My Or The At-Fault Party's Insurance Company Of The Accident?

It is certainly a good idea to notify your own insurance company when you're involved in an accident. This will protect your rights in the event that a case is brought against you. There are also many coverages that may be available to you on your own insurance policy, and if you don't notify them of the incident, then you won't be made aware of them.

It is best to hire a qualified personal injury attorney to contact the at-fault party's insurance on your behalf. All too often, injured parties provide an at-fault party's insurance company a recorded statement that ends up damaging their case.

What Happens If The At-Fault Driver Has Minimal Or No Insurance At All?

The minimum limit of insurance in Texas is $30,000 per person, which means the maximum amount the insurance company would be responsible for paying would be $30,000. However, your own insurance company may have uninsured or underinsured motorist coverage, which would protect you and anyone in your vehicle for damages that exceed $30,000. In the absence of insurance coverage, it may not be worthwhile to file a suit. Most people in Texas are judgment proof, which means that a judgment against them is not collectible. However, an attorney can determine if the party has assets that may be subject to collection.

After Filing A Claim, What Happens On The Insurance Company And At-Fault Party's Side?

After a claim has been filed, the insurance company will investigate the facts of the case. This investigation will include talking to all of the people who were involved in the accident and making an initial determination of liability. Depending on the complexity of the case, this process can be short or lengthy.

CHAPTER 9

WHY SHOULD I HIRE AN ATTORNEY EARLY ON IN A CASE?

Hiring an attorney is extremely important, especially if you are injured in an accident; the earlier you hire one the better. Insurance companies and adjusters are trained professionals and will use many tricks to avoid fairly compensating you for the injuries you suffered. Insurance companies will be celebrating if you don't hire an experienced personal injury attorney because that will immediately indicate to them that they can get away with paying you less than you're owed. In other words, an insurance company will take your case much more seriously if you hire an attorney. Unfortunately, many people have the misconception that the insurance company is there to help them and will be fair, but in reality, it is an insurance adjuster's job to pay you as little as possible.

In addition, there are lots of problems that could arise early on in a case without you even knowing it. For example, receiving improper medical attention or allowing any delay in treatment could be a death sentence for your case. It is much harder to fix a problem than it is to prevent one from occurring in the first place.

Once you hire an attorney, you should tell them everything about the case, as omitting or hiding any information could substantially hurt your case. For instance, quite recently I spoke to a client who gave an inaccurate description to one of his healthcare providers by saying that he injured his ankle at home when he had actually injured it in the accident; after being injured in the accident, he further injured his ankle at home. Since he didn't accurately describe his injury to the healthcare provider, his case was damaged.

How Do I Afford An Experienced Personal Injury Attorney?

Attorneys in personal injury cases typically work on a contingency fee basis, which means you won't have to pay anything until there is a successful settlement and/or judgment. This enables you to hire an attorney without the fear or burden of having to pay the attorney fee upfront. This also allows you to get the best possible personal injury attorney.

Things To Look For Or Avoid While Hiring A Personal Injury Attorney

There are many things to look for when hiring a personal injury attorney, such as whether they focus exclusively on personal injury law. You should not hire a criminal or divorce lawyer for your personal injury claim, just as you should not have an orthopedic surgeon treat a heart condition. You should also review a potential attorney's online reviews, length of time in practice, and reputation in the community.

If a lawyer makes immediate promises to you about your eventual recovery, run away; an attorney simply cannot know at the initial meeting the value of your case.

Instead, time and the extent of your injuries will be the deciding factors in the value of your case.

What Sets You And Your Firm Apart In Dealing With Personal Injury Cases In Texas?

I have been practicing law in El Paso, Texas since 1987. I grew up in El Paso and I have devoted lots of time and effort to helping our wonderful community. I believe in giving back to the community and have been paying it forward to the people of El Paso for many years. We have many different locations in El Paso and have an amazing and experienced staff to assist with your case. Our firm has the experience, the contacts, and the resources to obtain the results you deserve. Simply put, you'll be taken care of at the Law Offices of Michael Gopin.

INDEX

NOTES